A

Devotional

# A Christmas Devotional

Elmer Towns

DESTINY IMAGE® PUBLISHERS, INC.
P.O. Box 310, Shippensburg, PA 17257-0310
*"Promoting Inspired Lives."*

This book and all other Destiny Image and Destiny Image Fiction books are available at Christian bookstores and distributors worldwide.

For more information on foreign distributors, call 717-532-3040.
Reach us on the Internet: www.destinyimage.com.

ISBN 13 TP: 978-0-7684-6420-7
ISBN 13 eBook: 978-0-7684-6421-4

For Worldwide Distribution, Printed in the U.S.A.
1 2 3 4 5 6 7 8 / 27 26 25 24 23

# CONTENTS

# December 1
# Immanuel

*Call His name Immanuel, which is translated,*
*"God with us."* — Matthew 1:23

The angel told Joseph to name Me *Immanuel*, which means "God with us." When I was born, God visited humanity. I came to live with people and to die for their sins. I am God, even though many did not recognize Me. Today, I am still Immanuel, even when people don't feel My presence. Because I am with you, I can help you face your problems. I am with you, even when you don't realize I am near. However, you must call on Me, Immanuel, to get My help. I will be there when you need Me.

## Your Prayer

*Lord Jesus, there are many times I don't feel Your*
*presence. I want to feel Your nearness. I pray*
*about my problems, but they are still here. I know*
*You are by me. Manifest Yourself; help me*
*make it through my day. Amen.*

Because I am Immanuel, you can win when you let Me direct your efforts. I will give you hope when you feel like giving up. I will give you a courageous spirit to carry you through the rough spots. I will show you what to do and I will guide your steps. I will give you the tenacity to press on to victory. I am Immanuel with you; call on Me for help.

## Your Response

*Immanuel, I know You are with me. Help me
feel Your guiding presence this day. Release
Your indwelling power to do everything
I am supposed to do. I claim Your presence
for victory today. Amen.*

## DECEMBER 2

# THE FRUIT OF MARY'S WOMB

*Then she spoke out with a loud voice and said,
"Blessed are you among women, and blessed is the
fruit of your womb!"* — Luke 1:42

I am the *Fruit of Mary's womb*. The Holy Spirit supernaturally conceived Me in the virgin Mary, and nine months later
I was born in Bethlehem. I am eternal: "In the beginning
was the Word, and the Word was with God, and the Word
was God" (John 1:1). I "came forth from the Father" (John
16:28). While My spirit and personality came from Heaven,
My physical body came from Mary. I can rightly be called
the Fruit of Mary's womb. When Mary watched Me grow,
she saw her physical son developing. The Bible calls Me "her
firstborn Son" (Matthew 1:25).

## YOUR PRAYER

*Lord Jesus, thank You for becoming flesh to live as a
human being. Thank You for limiting Yourself to be
like finite people so You could die for them. Amen.*

I, the eternal God, became fully man. I, the man, was fully God. I was the God-man, always fully God and always fully man. While humans can't understand it, they read these apparent contradictions in the Bible and accept them both. They harmonize perfectly in Me. As a human, I felt tired, hungry, and thirsty. I didn't know who touched Me (see Mark 5:31), and I didn't know the date of My second coming (see Matthew 24:36), though I knew I was coming back. As God, I raised the dead (see Mark 5:38-42), calmed a storm (see Mark 6:47-51), and read people's thoughts (see Mark 2:8). What wonderful Fruit of Mary's womb!

## YOUR RESPONSE

*Lord Jesus, thank You for coming to Earth to be born of Mary; I will try to follow Your example as a man; I will worship You as God. Amen.*

## DECEMBER 3

# I AM JESUS, THE ONLY BEGOTTEN SON

*For God so loved the world that He gave His only begotten Son, that whoever believes in Him should not perish but have everlasting life.* — John 3:16

I am the Only Begotten Son, an Old Testament title declaring that I am eternally generated from the Father. The Father said to Me, "You are my Son, begotten throughout eternity" (Psalm 2:7). This does not mean that I was begotten at an event in eternity past; rather, it describes My eternal relationship to the Father. Both the Father and I are equally eternal and equally God, but we have separate personalities. We are equal in nature. I was not begotten at a time in the past, because that would mean I am not eternal. But the Father has eternally loved Me, and because the Father loves you and the world, He sent Me to die for your sins. When you receive Me as the Only Begotten Son, you have also believed in the Father.

## Your Prayer

*Jesus, I worship You just as I worship the Father.*
*You are both God, and I come into Your presence*
*with thanksgiving for all You've done for me. Amen.*

When you receive Me as Savior, you become a child of God (see Romans 8:14-16). The Father has only one Son who could die for the world, and because of that sacrificial death, the Father now has many "sons." You are a member of the family.

## Your Response

*Jesus, I worship You as the Only Begotten Son.*
*I praise You as the second Person of the Godhead.*
*I thank You for coming into the world to*
*die for my sins. Amen.*

# DECEMBER 4
# LORD JESUS CHRIST

*My brethren, do not hold the faith of our*
*Lord Jesus Christ, the Lord of glory, with partiality.*
— James 2:1

Christian people usually think of Me as having three names: "Lord," "Jesus," and "Christ." But these three names are entirely different from the first, middle, and last names that people have today. When you call Me Lord, that's My title. You are referring to My deity. No one gave Me the title "Lord," for I have eternally been Lord. When you call Me Jesus, you are referring to My humanity. The angel Gabriel told Mary to call Me Jesus, a Greek name that means "Jehovah saves." When you call Me Christ, you are referring to My anointed office. Just as prophets, priests, and kings were anointed into their office, so I came as Prophet to give the message of God, as Priest to bring salvation, and as King to rule the hearts of My followers.

## YOUR PRAYER

*I worship You as Christ, who brought me salvation;
as Jesus, the virgin-born son of Mary; and as my
King, who sits on the throne of my heart. Amen.*

Why do I, the Lord Jesus Christ have over 700 names, titles, and descriptive metaphors? It's because I am and do a vast number of things. Similarly, men who do many things have many titles (dad, husband, uncle, boss, deacon, and so on). But the names you call Me are not as important as your response to Me. I want your love and obedience.

## YOUR RESPONSE

*Jesus, You are my Redeemer, Intercessor,
Guide, Protector, and Friend. You came to me as
Light, Water, Bread, Shepherd, Vine,
and Resurrection. But most of all, You are my
Lord and my Savior. Amen.*

# December 5
# God with Us

*They shall call His name Immanuel, which is translated, "God with us."* Matthew 1:23

The angel told Joseph to name Me *Immanuel,* which means "God with us." When I was born, I, the Lord God, visited humanity. I came to live with people and die for their sins. I am God, even though many did not recognize Me. Today, I am still Immanuel, even when people don't feel My presence. Because I am with you, you can get Me to help you face your problems. I am with you, even when you don't realize I'm near. However, you must call on Immanuel to get My help. I am Immanuel, which means I'll be there when you need Me.

## Your Prayer

*Immanuel, there are many times I can't feel*
*Your presence. I want to feel Your nearness. I pray*
*about my problems, but they're still here.*
*I know You're by me. Manifest Yourself; help me*
*make it through my day. Amen.*

Because I'm Immanuel, you can win when you let Me direct your efforts. First, I will give you hope when you feel like giving up. Then I will give you a courageous spirit to carry you through the rough spots. Next, I will show you what to do and guide your steps. Finally, I'll give you the tenacity to press on to victory. Immanuel is with you, but you must call on Me to get help.

## YOUR RESPONSE

*Immanuel, I know You are with me. Help me feel Your guiding presence this day. Release Your indwelling power to do everything I'm supposed to do. I claim Your presence for victory today. Amen.*

## December 6
# The Young Child

*And when they had come into the house, they saw
the young Child with Mary His mother, and fell
down and worshiped Him. And when they had
opened their treasures, they presented gifts to Him:
gold, frankincense, and myrrh.* — Matthew 2:11

I was a young Child when the wise men came to Bethlehem to worship Me with gifts. The title "young Child" means more than a baby in arms. I was an infant, perhaps crawling or maybe even walking. This suggests there was a period of time between the shepherds' visit and the wise men's visit. It shouldn't surprise you that I, the young Child, grew (see Luke 2:40,52). That's what children do. It shouldn't surprise you what the wise men of understanding and position did: "They saw the young Child . . . and fell down and worshiped Him" (Matthew 2:11). Most people only cuddle young children or enjoy their antics; but if it's Me, you worship Me as God. What is your response to Me, the young Child?

## YOUR PRAYER

*Lord Jesus, I worship at Your feet because
You are God. But I also worship at Your feet
for what You did on the cross. Amen.*

The wise men worshipped Me, the young Child, with gifts: "And when they opened their treasures, they presented gifts to [Me]: gold, frankincense, and myrrh" (Matthew 2:11). Today, when you visit a newborn baby and family, you take a gift. You should do what the wise men did. Are you worshipping Me today?

## YOUR RESPONSE

*Lord Jesus, I come to worship, giving You my time,
my talent, and my treasure. But beyond these things,
I give You my greatest gift; I give You myself. Amen.*

## DECEMBER 7
# THE CHILD JESUS

*The parents brought in [to the temple] the Child
Jesus.... And the Child grew and became strong in
spirit, filled with wisdom; and the grace of God was
upon Him.* — Luke 2:27-40

I did not enter the world as a spirit; nor did I appear
instantly, as an angel may appear. I was supernaturally
conceived of a virgin and was born nine months later. My
development followed the growth pattern of other children: "And the Child grew and became strong in spirit,
filled with wisdom" (Luke 2:40). My parents had to teach
Me to walk and talk and develop motor skills. My parents
brought Me, the Child Jesus, to the temple to dedicate
Me. Then at age 12, I was brought into the temple for
My bar mitzvah and became a "son of the law." My parents raised Me according to the Scriptures, just as parents
should raise children today. I, the Son of God, was "born
under the law, to redeem those who were under the law"
(Galatians 4:4- 5).

## YOUR PRAYER

*Lord Jesus, I marvel that You became a child and grew according to the growth pattern of children. I praise You for becoming flesh to redeem us who were under the Law. Amen.*

God the Father sent Me to become a child who would grow into manhood. God the Holy Spirit guided Me as an adult: "Jesus, being filled with the Holy Spirit, returned from the Jordan and was led by the Spirit into the wilderness.... Then Jesus returned in the power of the Spirit to Galilee" (Luke 4:14). Both the Father and the Holy Spirit were active in bringing Me to maturity.

## YOUR RESPONSE

*Lord Jesus, You gave me a role model to follow; give me power to follow Your example. You died for my sins; I worship You for salvation. Amen.*

# DECEMBER 8

# THE SON OF MARY

*Is this not the carpenter, the Son of Mary,*
*and brother of James, Joseph, Judas, and*
*Simon? And are not His sisters here with us?*
— Mark 6:3

I am the Son of Mary, born as a human baby; yet My mother, Mary, was a virgin. Because she had not known a man, I was born sinless, without a sin nature. I lived My entire life without sin (see 2 Corinthians 5:21) so that I could be the unblemished substitute Lamb of God for the sins of the world. I, the Son of Mary, came to My own people—the Israelites—but they did not receive Me (see John 1:11). Even some members of My family were blinded to who I am (see John 7:5). When I preached to the people of My hometown, Nazareth, "they were offended at [Me]" (Mark 6:3). What is your response to Me? Will you be My disciple? Will you live blamelessly for Me?

## YOUR PRAYER

*Jesus, I believe You were 100 percent human, born of Mary; yet You are 100 percent God. Thank You for becoming human so You could understand us. I worship You, and I will follow Your example and strive to live godly. Amen.*

I, the Son of Mary, grew as a child and had favor with God and man (see Luke 2:52). My mother, Mary, taught Me lessons that a mother teaches her child. Now I want you to grow to please God as I did. "And the Child grew and became strong in spirit, filled with wisdom; and the grace of God was upon Him" (Luke 2:40).

## YOUR RESPONSE

*Jesus, I want You to live in my heart (see Galatians 2:20) to strengthen Me so that I can please the Father. Amen.*

## DECEMBER 9
# THE LAMB OF GOD

*Behold! The Lamb of God who takes away the sin of
the world!* — John 1:29

On the banks of the Jordan River, John the Baptist announced to the world, "Behold! The Lamb of God." For hundreds of years, thousands of faithful Israelites sacrificed millions of lambs—all looking forward to the coming of the Messiah, who would forgive their sins. Because I am the Lamb of God, all the drudgery of sacrifice finally came to an end. Now, every new day should be exciting because I, the Lamb of God, have taken away the sin of the world—including all of yesterday's mistakes. I have taken away your sins because you believed in Me. Today is a new opportunity to serve Me. Be thankful for the Lamb who has taken away your sins.

## YOUR PRAYER

*O Lamb of God, forgive me for the willful sins I do,
and look deeply to see my repentance. Purge me of
the ignorant sins I don't realize I do. Amen.*

Learn to worship Me, the Lamb. Learn to do on Earth what you'll do in Heaven. Worship should be your passion now, since you will worship once you arrive in Heaven. When you get to Heaven, you will join many others who are worshipping "Him who sits on the throne, and to the Lamb, forever and ever!" (Revelation 5:13). In Heaven you will cry out with others, "Worthy is the Lamb who was slain" (Revelation 5:12).

## YOUR RESPONSE

*Jesus, Lamb of God, at Your name I join every*
*knee bowing and every tongue confessing*
*that You, Jesus Christ, are Lord*
*(see Philippians 2:10-11). Amen.*

# December 10
# The Word

*In the beginning was the Word, and the Word was*
*with God, and the Word was God.* — John 1:1

I am Jesus, the Word. As the Word, I expressed the true idea of the Father, just as a written word represents the ideas of an author. I am also called the Word because I am the One who communicated the Father's desires to people, just as a written word communicates an author's intent. I am also the Word because I interpret the Father to the world, just as a human author interprets a theme to readers. Words are symbols of meaning, and I am the symbol that showed the world what God was like in the flesh.

## Your Prayer

*Jesus, I look to You to show me what God is like.*
*I will study the Word of God to better understand*
*You and know what You expect of me. Amen.*

I am the powerful Word who lived in the flesh. My spoken words were also powerful, for My words raised the dead, calmed storms, and comforted the hurting. My written Word is just as powerful as My spoken words. The written Word can save, heal, cast out demons, and become the basis for answered prayer (see Colossians 3:16; Hebrews 4:12). I elevated My words to a supernatural level when I said, "The words that I speak to you are spirit, and they are life" (John 6:63). Peter agreed with Me when he said, "You have the words of eternal life" (John 6:68).

## YOUR RESPONSE

*Lord Jesus, I love Your Word because You tell me about the Father. I love Your words because they are spirit and life. Amen.*

# December 11
# Son of Joseph

*Philip found Nathanael and said to him, "We have found Him of whom Moses in the law, and also the prophets, wrote—Jesus of Nazareth, the son of Joseph."* — John 1:45

I am called the Son of Joseph because Joseph was My earthly stepfather and legal guardian. Therefore you are technically right calling Me the Son of Joseph. I was conceived by the Holy Spirit in the Virgin Mary when Joseph was engaged to her. Joseph could have legally annulled the engagement, but when an angel explained My supernatural birth, he married Mary (see Matthew 1:18-25). Joseph endured the embarrassing rumors that I had been conceived out of wedlock (see John 8:41). As an earthly father, Joseph protected Me, provided for Me, taught Me the trade of carpentry, and guided My youth into manhood.

## YOUR PRAYER

*Jesus, You are the Son of Joseph. You are the Son of
God. I will follow You and worship You.*

Philip told his friend that I was the Son of Joseph (see
John 1:45). Are you willing to tell others who I am? Because Philip was a faithful witness, his friend Nathaniel
became one of My 12 disciples. When Nathaniel had
questions about Me, Philip simply said, "Come and see"
(John 1:46). Tell your friends about Me. When they have
questions, tell them to look at Me and I will answer their
questions. When your friends see who I am, they will
follow Me as you do.

## YOUR RESPONSE

*Jesus, I know You are human, born of a virgin, the
Son of Joseph. But I also know You are the eternal
Son of God. I will learn from You and tell my
friends what I've learned. I will worship You and be
transformed by Your presence. Amen.*

# DECEMBER 12
# SON OF THE HIGHEST

*He will be great, and will be called the Son of the Highest; and the Lord God will give Him the throne of His father David.* — Luke 1:32

I am the Son of the Highest, as no human can be. The name "Most High" in the original Hebrew language means *El Elyon*, which means "Possessor of heaven and earth" (Genesis 14:19). Originally, Lucifer wanted to be "like the Most High [God]" (Isaiah 14:14), the ruler of Heaven and Earth. Notice the word "like." Lucifer could never have become the actual Most High God; that is a title and position that only God can possess. Since I am Jesus, the Father's Son, I am the Son of the Highest, or the Son of the Most High. One of the many reasons to worship the Father is because He possesses Heaven and Earth. Therefore, worship Me, because I am the Son of the Highest.

## YOUR PRAYER

*Jesus, I worship You as the Son of the Highest. Rule my heart today, just as You rule Heaven and Earth. Amen.*

The heavenly Father is *El Elyon,* who possesses all things, which He gives to Me. When I sent My disciples out to serve, I said, "All authority has been given to Me in heaven and on earth" (Matthew 28:18). I send you to serve Me today with the same authority. "Go make disciples" (Matthew 28:19). My promise to you is that "I am with you always" (Matthew 28:20). So serve Me with confidence, knowing you have My power and presence with you today.

## YOUR RESPONSE

*Jesus, it is thrilling to know that You, the Son of the Highest, will be with me today. Use me in Your service; give me the power of Your authority and presence. Amen.*

## DECEMBER 13

# ONLY BEGOTTEN OF THE FATHER

*And the Word became flesh and dwelt among us,*
*and we beheld His glory, the glory as of the only*
*begotten of the Father, full of grace and truth.*
— John 1:14

I am the Only Begotten of the Father, which means I came from the Father and I am the unique personification of the Father. I being begotten of the Father means that I am the expression of the Father. John 1:14 emphasizes My characteristics of being "the Word," which means that the message and meaning of the Word reflect the Father. When the Father wants to make an utterance to the world, He does it through Me, the Word.

## YOUR PRAYER

*Lord Jesus, I come asking You to teach me what the*
*Father in Heaven is like. I want to love the Father*

*more than ever, but I must know Him better to love*
*Him better. Amen.*

I am the Only Begotten of the Father, which means, I am just like the Father. If you want to see what the Father is like, look at Me in the Scriptures. If you want to know how the Father relates to you, look at how I relate to people. If you want to approach the Father, go to Him through Me. To know the Father better, know Me.

## YOUR RESPONSE

*Lord Jesus, I look to You to see the Father. I know*
*the Father is loving because I see how You loved*
*people. I know the Father is powerful because I see*
*Your awesome power in creating the universe and in*
*transforming individuals. I know the Father is kind*
*and gentle because You are patient with me and*
*forgiving toward me. Amen.*

# December 14
# Savior

*For there is born to you this day in the city of David*
*a Savior, who is Christ the Lord.* — Luke 2:11

I am Jesus the Savior, the title that means "deliverer" or
"preserver." I have many names, but the most important
name may be "Savior," because I am the only One who
can save you. "Salvation is of the LORD" (Jonah 2:9). I
am the Savior who will deliver you in many ways. I have
saved you from the guilt of past sin and from the present
bondage of sin, and I will save you from the future penal-
ty of sin. When you die, I will take you to Heaven.

## Your Prayer

*Lord Jesus, You have done so many things for me—*
*things I don't even realize. But Your most*
*important gift was saving me; thank You. I feel*
*confident in Your salvation, yet I want more. I want*
*to enjoy all the benefits possible that come*
*from salvation. Amen.*

I am Jesus, the Savior (see 2 Peter 1:1). John referred to Me as "Savior of the world" (1 John 4:14). The Caesars of the Roman Empire called themselves the saviors of the world, but they could only give military deliverance. I came to save you from damnation and eternal death. I will save you from weaknesses, temptations, attacks from Satan, and addiction to sin. I will save all those who come to Me.

## Your Response

*I praise You, Savior, for "so great a salvation" (Hebrews 2:3). You have saved me in so many ways; continue to save me to the very end. Amen.*

## DECEMBER 15

# NAME ABOVE ALL OTHER NAMES

*Therefore God also has highly exalted Him and
given Him the name which is above every name.*
— Philippians 2:9

My name, Jesus, is a name above every name. It is more
excellent than that of Adam, the first man, because I am
the Alpha and the Omega. My name is more excellent
than that of Noah, who saved the world from the flood,
because I will save the world from fire in the future. My
name is more excellent than that of Abraham, the friend
of God, because I am God's Son. My name is more excellent than that of Moses, who delivered Israel from slavery
in Egypt, because My name is powerful to deliver any
from addictive slavery to sin. My name is more excellent
than that of any judge who defeated Israel's enemies, because I defeated sin, lust, and the devil on the cross. What
has My name done for you?

## Your Prayer

*When I'm in trouble, I whisper, "Jesus."
When I want to break a habit or overcome an
enemy, I say, "Jesus." When I need anything,
I pray, "Jesus." Amen.*

My name, Jesus, is greater than that of every Old Testament prophet, priest, or king, because I am the focus of their ministry. My name, Jesus, is greater than every apostle, including Paul, because I called them, empowered them, commissioned them, and used them. What My name has done for these, I can do for you.

## Your Response

*Jesus, Your name is sweet to me, for it saved me
from sin. Your name is powerful to me, for
it gives me strength and hope. Your name is above
every name. Amen.*

## December 16
# The Name of Jesus

*Whatever you do in word or deed, do all in the
name of the Lord Jesus.* — Colossians 3:17

There's power in My name, Jesus. Remember that signs
and wonders are done through My name, Jesus (see Acts
4:30). My name, Jesus, cleansed the lepers and opened
the eyes of the blind, and I can do what you need done
today. Don't forget that I can get your prayers answered
in My name, Jesus: "If you ask anything in My name, I
will do it" (John 14:14).

## Your Prayer

*Jesus, give me discipline to overcome my weaknesses,
power to overcome opposition, and strength to
overcome disappointments. Jesus, I claim the
strength of Your name to rid my life of all evil lusts.
By Your name, deliver me from the evil one
(see Matthew 6:13). Amen.*

My name, Jesus, can fix broken lives and can heal sickness. A man had never walked, but My name made him strong (see Acts 3:16). My name, Jesus, can dispel evil powers. A girl was released from a demon when Paul said, "In the name of Jesus Christ come out" (See Acts 16:18). My name, Jesus, can transform your life and ministry. So do everything today in My name. Remember, "Whatever you do in word or deed, do all in the name of the Lord Jesus" (Colossians 3:17). What can My name, Jesus, do for you?

## YOUR RESPONSE

*Jesus, Your name is sweet; it gives me joy. Jesus,*
*Your name is comforting; it gives me assurance.*
*Jesus, Your name is powerful; I claim Your*
*strength to overcome barriers. Jesus, Your name is*
*awesome; I worship Your name. Amen.*

# December 17

# Most Excellent

*Having become so much better than the angels, as
He has by inheritance obtained a more excellent
name than they.* — Hebrews 1:4

I, Jesus, have a More Excellent Name than the angels. I sent the angels as ministering spirits to help you as an heir of salvation (see Hebrews 1:14), but I, Jesus, was sent to purchase your salvation. I have a More Excellent Name than Moses, who led Israel out of Egypt and gave the Israelites the Law (see Hebrews 3:3). I fulfilled the Law and died to take it out of the way (see Colossians 2:13-15). I have a More Excellent Name than the high priest, who interceded for Israel (see Hebrews 4:14-16). I give you grace, for which the high priest prayed. I have a More Excellent Name than Melchizedek, because I obtained a better salvation and a new covenant (see Hebrews 7:22-24). Because of the excellence of My name, you can go to the Father through Me at any time. Will you pray to the Father through My name?

## Your Prayer

*Jesus, I love Your name. Your name calms my fears
and guides me each day. Jesus, Your name saved me
and Your name keeps me safe. Amen.*

Because I, Jesus, have a More Excellent Name, you can pray in My name (see John 14:13-14). Because My name has power, you can break addiction and cast out demonic powers in My name (see Acts 16:18). Because My name sets prisoners free, you can have a powerful witness to the unsaved in My name (see Acts 16:10-14). One day, every knee will bow to recognize and worship My name, Jesus (see Philippians 2:9-11). Will you do it now?

## Your Response

*Jesus, I worship at the sound of Your name.
You are worthy to receive all honor, praise,
and thanksgiving. Amen.*

## DECEMBER 18
# WORTHY

*Worthy is the Lamb who was slain to receive power
and riches and wisdom, and strength and honor
and glory and blessing!* — Revelation 5:12

I am worthy to receive your worship for two extraordinary reasons: First, worship Me because I am the omnipotent Creator, "and without Me nothing was made that was made" (John 1:3). I have given you life, purpose, and existence, because you were created in My image. Because of My creative act at the beginning of the world, all created beings—angels and redeemed souls—cry out in praise and adoration to Me. Have you given Me praise and adoration on Earth?

## YOUR PRAYER

*Lord Jesus, I cry, "Holy, holy, holy," for Your
awesome power that created me. You are worthy to
receive my praise for Your saving grace,
which redeemed me. Amen.*

I am worthy for another reason: My sacrificial death for all people and My specific pardon of your sin. I was not worthy of a cruel death, but still I chose to die for you. I am the One with great glory and power in Heaven. I am worthy of even more adoration because I purchased redemption on the cross. John wept because he thought no one was worthy to open and read the scroll, the title deed to Heaven and Earth. But I, the Lord, stepped forth to do it, because I am qualified to do so (see Revelation 5:4,8-10). That makes Me worthy of all praise in Heaven and Earth.

## YOUR RESPONSE

*Lord Jesus, I fall down at Your feet to cry, "Worthy is the Lamb," because You created all things. You are worthy to open the scroll because You redeemed me. Amen.*

# DECEMBER 19
# THE MIGHTY GOD

*For unto us a Child is born, unto us a Son is given;*
*and the government will be upon His shoulder.*
*And His name will be called Wonderful, Counselor,*
*Mighty God, Everlasting Father, Prince of Peace.*
— Isaiah 9:6

Wonderful things happen to those who recognize Me as the Mighty God and who call upon Me. When people refuse to recognize Me as their Mighty God, I cannot bless them, for they have shut the spiritual window of their life. But to those who have yielded their lives to Me, I can be their Mighty God. Everything promised in Scripture can happen to you, because I am mighty to bless those who have faith to receive it. What is your greatest desire today? "Delight thyself also in the LORD; and he shall give thee the desires of thine heart" (Psalm 37:4 KJV).

## Your Prayer

*Lord Jesus, I recognize Your might, but my problem is outward. I don't have enough faith to trust You to do mighty things in my life. I believe in my head; overcome the unbelief of my heart. Amen.*

I am the Mighty God to answer prayer. I am also the Mighty God to overcome bad habits and to give you strength to resist temptation. I am the Mighty God to give you peace in the middle of a storm. I can take you off of your wayward path and give you purpose in life. I transform from the inside out. If you need a spiritual makeover, call on Me, your Mighty God.

## Your Response

*Jesus, be mighty to discipline my thoughts.*
*Be mighty to focus my emotions in worship to You.*
*Be mighty to strengthen my will against temptation.*
*Be mighty to use my body as Your temple. Amen.*

# DECEMBER 20
# THE LIGHT

*Then Jesus spoke to them again, saying, "I am the light of the world. He who follows Me shall not walk in darkness, but have the light of life."*
— John 8:12

I am Jesus, the light. I can show you where to walk today. I was the light that shined into your heart before you were saved so that you were convicted of your sin and repented. I was the light that pointed you to salvation. Today, I'll be your light to show you what to do as you walk through the many decisions that you face. I am a bright shining light. I can enlighten you through the Scriptures, but you must study them. I can help you see clearly as you pray, but you must seek My presence. I can give you light to make better decisions, but you must make time for communion with Me.

## Your Prayer

*Jesus, take away my spiritual blindness. Help me see*
*what I must do today. Don't let me stumble or get*
*lost. Shine light on my path.*

I am the light of salvation. You may stumble when you walk outside the perimeter of My light, so always take Me, your light, with you. Let My light shine, giving you illumination when you don't know what to do. You can always have the blessings of light when you take Me with you.

## Your Response

*Jesus, help me make better choices; keep me*
*from making mistakes. Be light to help me*
*understand my friends and associates at work.*
*Shine on me when I walk through dark, threatening*
*valleys. Lord, thank You for the warmth*
*of your light. I feel comfortable in Your presence.*
*Keep me from stumbling in the night.*
*Keep me in the light. Amen.*

## DECEMBER 21

# THE GREAT SHEPHERD

*Now may the God of peace who brought up our
Lord Jesus from the dead, that great Shepherd of the
sheep, through the blood of the everlasting covenant.*
— Hebrews 13:20

There are many roles for the Great Shepherd of the Sheep.
I am the Shepherd who takes care of you (see Psalm 23:1).
All that the sheep have to do to receive My care is to keep
in good relationship with Me. I am the Good Shepherd
who gave My life for the sheep (see John 10:11). Just as
a shepherd sacrifices his family time and the comforts of
home to be with his sheep, so too I gave up Heaven for
you. I am also the Great Shepherd who said, "I lay down
My life" (John 10:17).

## YOUR PRAYER

*Lord Jesus, You are my Shepherd who has died for
my sins. You are my Shepherd who leads me daily
and takes care of me. Amen.*

I am also called the Great Shepherd of the Sheep because I safely deliver My sheep to Heaven. The basis for the complete and final salvation of My sheep is first My blood, which forgives the sheep, and second My resurrection, "The Lord Jesus from the dead" (Hebrews 13:20), which gives eternal life to the sheep. Because salvation is complete, I can "make you complete in every good work to do [My] will" (Hebrews 13:21). That means you can complete My will. How can that happen? Because I, the Great Shepherd of the Sheep, work "in you what is well pleasing in His [the Father's] sight" (Hebrews 13:21).

## YOUR RESPONSE

*Lord Jesus, I am complete in You. You have taken away all my sins. You have given me eternal life. You have worked in my life to help me please the Father. Amen.*

## DECEMBER 22

# THE MAN CHILD

*And she brought forth a man child, who was to rule all nations with a rod of iron; and her child was caught up unto God, and to his throne.*
— Revelation 12:5 KJV

I am called the Man Child because I was born as a child to live as a man and die for the sins of the world. When Mary and Joseph first saw Me, I was a baby in the manger, but the heavenly Father always saw Me as a fully grown man hanging on the cross, because I was born the Man Child to die for sins. But I was more than one man who died; I was every man, because, on the cross, all mankind was identified in Me on the cross. Just as all died in Adam, so too all were made alive in Me (see 1 Corinthians 15:22). I was more than just one man hanging on the cross; I was you, because I became your sin-bearer. Your sins were on Me when I died.

## Your Prayer

*Lord Jesus, I thank You for being born as a child, growing to be a man, and then dying for me. Thank You for giving me eternal life. Amen.*

Satan knew that I was the promised Man Child who would deliver the world, so throughout the Old Testament, Satan tried to eliminate the Jews so that I wouldn't be born. He tried to prematurely kill Me so I wouldn't die on the cross. But I prevailed for you; so today will you live for Me?

## Your Response

*Lord Jesus, You understand the pressures of life because You lived as a man. You were tried, hurt, and disappointed. You know what it's like to be tempted because You overcame temptation. Help me overcome my temptations and limitations today. Amen.*

# DECEMBER 23
# THE MAN

*Then Jesus came out, wearing the crown of thorns*
*and the purple robe. And Pilate said to them,*
*"Behold the Man!"* — John 19:5

I am the Man whom the Jewish leaders brought to the Roman governor Pilate to be tried. They said when I claimed to be God, "He [had] spoken blasphemy!" (Matthew 26:65). Pilate interrogated Me but found no crime in Me. Still the Jews cried out for My blood. So Pilate had Me flogged with whips and sticks. The Roman governor wrongly thought that a brutal beating would satisfy the bloodthirsty crowd. Then Pilate presented Me to them, exclaiming, "Behold the Man!" (John 19:5). When he called Me "the Man," perhaps Pilate thought the crowd would go way when they saw Me brutally beaten. But instead they cried, "Crucify Him!" What do you cry when you see Me, the Man?

## YOUR PRAYER

*Lord Jesus, I repent of my sins when I see Your
sufferings. I cry out for forgiveness and mercy.
You are the Son of God. Amen.*

I am the Man who was tried by a Roman court. I am the
Man who died for your sins. I am the Man who inter-
cedes for you at the right hand of the Father in Heaven.
I am the Man who will return from Heaven to judge the
world. I am the Man who also is God.

## YOUR RESPONSE

*Jesus, I worship You for Your great divine glory
because I don't understand why You would become a
Man to die for me. I bow in human amazement at
Your greatness. Amen.*

# December 24

# The Unspeakable Gift

*Thanks be unto God for his unspeakable gift.*
— 2 Corinthians 9:15 KJV

I am the unspeakable gift. Receive Me as you would receive any gift. Remember, a gift is free; if you have to work for it, it's not a gift. You can't pay for a gift; you can't work for a gift and put it on your credit card. All you can do is receive a gift. I am the unspeakable gift of salvation; receive Me freely.

## Your Prayer

*Lord Jesus, I receive You into my heart. I am saved by grace through faith, not by works; salvation is Your gift to me (see Ephesians 2:8-9). Your gift is greater than anything in life. Teach me to appreciate my salvation and to live accordingly. Amen.*

I am the unspeakable gift. Words are not adequate to describe Me. I am greater than the human mind can conceive and more precious than the human heart desires. Human words can't adequately express the worth of My salvation. I am the unspeakable gift, greater than anything on Earth. Any financial gain does not compare to My riches. Any good for which you strive cannot compare to the satisfaction of finding Me and making Me the center of your life. Be thankful for the unspeakable gift of My salvation.

## YOUR RESPONSE

*Lord Jesus, my words are not adequate to express my feelings, so look within my heart to receive the worship that is there. And when my words of worship are not adequate, look deeper in my heart to discover my love for You. Amen.*

# December 25

# The Babe

*And this will be the sign to you: You will find a Babe wrapped in swaddling cloths, lying in a manger.* — Luke 2:12

I am the Babe born in Bethlehem, the One born to a virgin. I did not come in a spaceship or by some aberrant or bizarre entrance into the world. I existed throughout eternity past, but I "became flesh" (John 1:14) and came as a little baby into the world. I needed a mother to care and love Me, just as any other child does. I played with other children and learned lessons at Mary's knee. Because I was human, I know your problems. Will you talk to Me about them?

## Your Prayer

*Lord Jesus, because You became human, You know how weak I am. I need strength to stand as a Christian in a non-Christian world. I need strength to keep on living for You. Amen.*

I am the Babe who grew in "wisdom and stature, and in favor with God and men" (Luke 2:52), so I know how you must grow both physically and spiritually. Because I am the Babe of Bethlehem, I can identify with your weaknesses and help you overcome them. "He learned obedience by the things which He suffered" (Hebrews 5:8); therefore, I can help you through your pain and problems. Look to Me for help.

## YOUR RESPONSE

*Lord Jesus, I have never been spat upon for being a Christian, nor have I been beaten or nailed to a cross. But I face many hardships. Life is difficult; can You help me? I look to Your human example; I'm trusting Your inner strength. Amen.*

# TALKING TO JESUS ON A
# FIRST-NAME BASIS

Elmer Towns knows a lot about the names of Jesus. He has lectured on His many names and wrote three best-selling books: *The Names of Jesus, My Father's Names*, and *The Names of the Holy Spirit*. This last book, *The Names of the Holy Spirit*, won the Gold Medallion award for the best book on Bible study from the Christian Booksellers Association in 1995. He also has compiled the most extensive list of the names of God. Now he has written these 25 daily devotions.

These Christmas devotionals are called *Talking to Jesus on a First-Name Basis* because they contain prayers for you to talk to Jesus using one of His personal names each day. This booklet can be an exciting 25-day journey into knowing Jesus more intimately through His many names.

In this devotional Elmer Towns writes to our hearts so that we can feel and apply Jesus to our everyday living. Through His name we can touch Jesus, but most importantly He can touch us.

# ABOUT ELMER TOWNS

ELMER L. TOWNS is co-founder of Liberty University with Jerry Falwell Sr. in 1971, and former Dean of the School of Religion and Liberty Baptist Theological Seminary. Each Sunday he continues to teach the Pastor's Bible Class at Thomas Road Baptist Church, which is televised on a local network and Angel One.

# In the Right Hands, This Book Will Change Lives!

Most of the people who need this message will not be looking for this book. To change their lives, you need to **put a copy of this book in their hands.**

Our ministry is constantly seeking methods to find the people who need this anointed message to change their lives. **Will you help us reach these people?**

**Extend this ministry by sowing 3 books, 5 books, 10 books, or more today, and become a life changer!** Your generosity will be part of catalyzing the Great Awakening that many have been prophesying and praying for.

From

# ELMER L. TOWNS

## The Bible is the only answer that can satisfy the longing of every human heart

*The Bible by Jesus* is a unique presentation of the Scriptures from the perspective of Jesus the Author Himself. This powerful paraphrase of the Old and New Testaments will usher you into a fresh level of intimate experience with God through His Word.

You will see Christ in every book of the Bible. Then you will understand Scripture that transforms your life.

- Encounter the Old Testament as a gateway to know Jesus.
- Read to hear the voice of Jesus speaking through the Gospel as He tells you of His birth, ministry, death and resurrection.
- Experience Acts, the epistles, and the book of Revelation to know Jesus and His will for our life.

Read the pages of Scripture to hear the Son of God Himself and draw near to encounter His presence.

## Purchase your copy wherever books are sold

From
# ELMER L. TOWNS

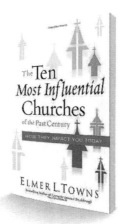

## Your Church Can Influence the World

History has shown that great leaders have the ability to reach beyond the walls of their churches to influence cultures for Christ. We've seen it in the Pentecostal/Charismatic movement, in the explosive growth of house churches in Communist China, in the expansion of the Southern Baptist Convention, and in the world-wide rise of praise and worship music led by Hillsong Church, among other phenomena.

In *The Ten Most Influential Churches of the Past Century*, Dr. Elmer Towns presents evidence of the powerful influence of these churches and how their innovative strategies and faith accomplish these goals. Then he tells how you can apply these principles to your church. You will learn how some of the most influential leaders in Church history became conduits for your future ministry and how your church can experience exponential growth.

Most importantly, you will see that the great results in these ten churches grow out of the power of the Word of God, the ministry of many dedicated lay workers, the faith-producing ministry of great leaders—all under the anointing of the Holy Spirit.

## Purchase your copy wherever books are sold

From
# ELMER L. TOWNS

The Book of Psalms reflects the heart of God. *Praying the Psalms* carefully shapes the Psalms into personal prayers enabling you to identify with the Psalmist as he prayed. The author, Dr. Towns, is living breathing testimony of the power and fulfillment you will experience as you read the pages of this most powerful book.

The Psalmist poured our his soul to God concerning the things that deeply moved him. As you read the Psalms, you are taking a peak into his heart. You will weep when he weeps, should when he rejoices, burn when he gets angry and fall on your face when he worships God.

## Purchase your copy wherever books are sold

From
# ELMER L. TOWNS

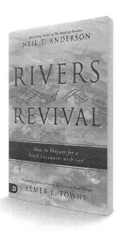

Since the Day of Pentecost, seasons of revival and awakening have brought refreshing to the spiritually dry, life to the spiritually dead, and miraculous encounters with the Holy Spirit.

In this timely and prophetic volume, two bestselling generals of the faith, Dr. Elmer Towns and Dr. Neil T. Anderson, offer collective wisdom, insight, and strategy on how you can experience and release a river of Holy Spirit outpouring into your world!

Additionally, Drs. Towns and Anderson have compiled contributions from other key authorities on revival who have encountered the move of God firsthand. Each contributor provides practical wisdom on how you can experience the Spirit's touch in your own life, church and even geographical region.

A fresh move of God is on the way. Prepare yourself to experience Holy Spirit outpouring like never before!

## Purchase your copy wherever books are sold

Made in the USA
Columbia, SC
12 October 2023

24385403R00037